YOUR KNOWLEDGE HAS VALUE

Bibliographic information published by the German National Library:

The German National Library lists this publication in the National Bibliography; detailed bibliographic data are available on the Internet at http://dnb.dnb.de .

Imprint:

Copyright © 2017 GRIN Verlag, Open Publishing GmbH
Print and binding: Books on Demand GmbH, Norderstedt Germany
ISBN: 9783668487437

This book at GRIN:

http://www.grin.com/en/e-book/366654/corporate-finance-summary-about-company-valuation-and-taxation-in-general

Mike G.

Corporate Finance. Summary about company valuation and taxation in general

GRIN Publishing

GRIN - Your knowledge has value

Since its foundation in 1998, GRIN has specialized in publishing academic texts by students, college teachers and other academics as e-book and printed book. The website www.grin.com is an ideal platform for presenting term papers, final papers, scientific essays, dissertations and specialist books.

Visit us on the internet:

http://www.grin.com/

http://www.facebook.com/grincom

http://www.twitter.com/grin_com

Lecture Transcript

~ Corporate Finance ~

This text is about a six-session-long lecture about the principles and advances in corporate finance. Two different professors taught about company valuation and taxation in general. Not only the transcript of the lecturers' speech, but also the board notes (captured in self-made pictures and tables) and some information from secondary literature / newspaper articles are included. It was composed for an upcoming exam for preparation purposes and, therefore, a summary of this content is added at the end. However, it is not only useful for exams, it also allows the reader to get a better knowledge about the basic principles ad theories of corporate finance.

- **Goals and Governance of the firm.**
  - Two main financial decisions are: Where to get the money from (fund raising) and where to invest in (investment).
- → Typically separated but actually have many points in common.
  - Investments can be find on the asset side of the balance sheet (+ OBS items and intangibles), raised funds on the right hand side.
  - To make investors invest, you must provide an adequate return to meet their opportunity costs.
    - Adequate means in comparison with similar investments, similar in maturity, liquidity and risk.
  - Three major company types.

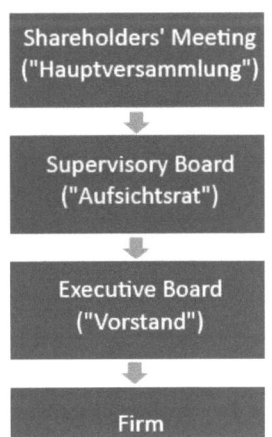

- **Sole Proprietorship**: One individual running the business, owner is manager and personal liable, no conflicts of interest.
- **Partnership**: Similar to sole proprietorship, but consists of multiple owners.
- **Corporation**: Stockholders are the managers, which leads to potential conflicts of interest (→ moral hazard).

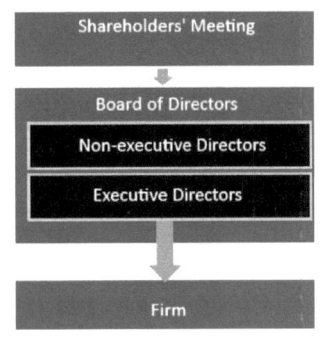

- **One Tier System vs. Two Tier System.**
  - **Two-tier board.**
    - **Shareholders' Meeting** elects the **Supervisory Board**,

which elects the **Executive Board** consisting of the managers running the company.

- Employee representatives are elected and become part of the supervisory board.
- Try to reduce the moral hazard, but doesn't ensure the implementation of shareholders' interests.
  - **One-tier board.**
    - The **Shareholders' Meeting** elects the **Board of Directors** consisting of internal directors and external directors (with advisory tasks) ruling the firm.
    - External directors should take care about the implementation of shareholders' interests, but don't have those deep insights into the company, as the internal directors have.

- **Shareholders vs. Stakeholders.**
  - Stakeholders have interest in the firm, Shareholders own parts of the firm.
  - Both have cash flow and control rights.
    - In case of receiving dividends, bond holders are preferred over shareholders, but in case of controlling it's the other way round.
    - Bond holders only have a right to say in case of illiquidity of the firm.
  - But the management should take care about the stakeholders → CSR.
  - International differences in company orientation.
    - Companies like Japan, France and Germany focus (very) much on stakeholders value whereas the Anglo-Saxon countries focus more on the shareholders value (due to Adam Smith?).
    - Japan implemented employee loyalty by offering many perks as reaction of high mobility of specialists.

- **Duties of the financial managers.**
  - Take care about the raise and use of funds, but also of the distribution of profits (reinvest or dividend).
  - Major fields of action of a CFO are treasury and controlling.
    - **Treasury**: Cash management, raising and usage of funds, etc.
    - **Controlling**: Accounting book keeping.

- **Valuation of Stocks.**
  - Characteristics of a common stock.
    - Right for dividends as cash or share dividends.
    - Payouts are uncertain in both magnitude and timing.
    - Stockholders have limited liabilities as well as the four basic shareholder rights.

- **Distinguish the primary and secondary market.**
  - **Primary market** deals with new shares.
    - IPO / SEO, Venture Capital or deals with investment banks acting as underwriters.
  - **Secondary markets** deal with the trade of already existing shares.
    - Organized exchanges like NYSE or OTC-Transactions.
- **Importance of stock valuation.**
  - Risk determines price and return.
  - Market price doesn't reflect all information.
  - Understand the key determinants of the stock price.
- **Valuate stocks by key ratios.**
  - Determine important key ratios (like price-earning ratio) for firms which are calculated to be very similar.
  - The lowest P/E Ratio reveals a convergence to the average.
  - High P/E ratio represents expectation of high future cash flows.
- **Formulae for expected return and price determination.**
  - **Single period consideration.**

$$\text{Expected return} = r = \frac{Div_1 + P_1 - P_0}{P_0} \qquad \text{Price} = P_0 = \frac{Div_1 + P_1}{1 + r}$$

  - $r = \frac{D_1 + P_1}{P_0} - \frac{P_0}{P_0} \rightarrow r + 1 = \frac{D_1 + P_1}{P_0} \rightarrow P_0 = \frac{D_1 + P_1}{r + 1}$.

  - **Multiple period consideration.**

    - Dividend Discount Model.

$$P_0 = \sum_{t=1}^{H} \frac{Div_t}{(1 + r)^t} + \frac{P_H}{(1 + r)^H}$$

    - Applying this model to 100 periods

    reveals that only 1,17% of the present value is determined by the future price.

→ In infinity, the present value of stocks equals the sum of discounted dividends.

    - Therefore the short formula for infinity is:

$$P_0 = \sum_{t=1}^{\infty} \frac{Div_t}{(1 + r)^t}$$

    - $P_1 = PV(Div_2) + PV(Div_3) + \dots + PV(Div_H)$.
    - $P_H = PV(Div_{h+1}) + \dots + PV(Div_\infty)$.

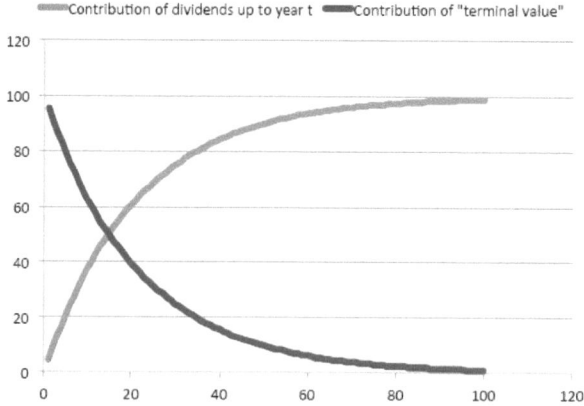

Contribution of dividends up to year t — Contribution of "terminal value"

- **Relevant shortcut formulae.**

  ○ $PerpetuityP = \frac{1}{r}$.

  ○ $t - periodperpetuityP = \frac{1}{r} - \frac{1}{r*(1+r)^t}$ If dividend payout ratio fluctuates for t periods.

  ○ $GrowingperpetuityP = \frac{1}{r-g}$ If payout ratio grows by g% each period.

  ○ $t - periodgrowingperpetuityP = \frac{1}{r-g} * \left[1 - \frac{(1+g)^t}{(1+r)^t}\right]$ If growth fluctuates for t periods.

- **Cost of Equity Capital.**

  ○ Normally actual price and future dividends are given, therefore calculate the cost of equity.

  → Opportunity costs of equity holders.

  ○ $r = \frac{\text{Div}_1}{P_0} + g$ Cost of Equity = Dividend Yield + Growth Rate (all percentages).

  ○ Several ways to compute the equity costs.

  ▪ **(1) Estimate the dividend yield.**

  • Relatively easy since the dividends mainly stay constant over time and therefore can be calculated quickly.

  ▪ **(2) Estimate the growth rate.**

  • (2.1) Ask experts: Companies like Value Line or IBES forecast the growth rate of several firms and can be asked for data.

  • (2.2) Calculate growth by plowback ratio and RoE.

  ○ G = RoE * Plowback Ratio.

  ▪ $plowbackratio = 1 - paybackratio = 1 - \frac{\text{Div}}{\text{EPS}}$.

- $RoE = \dfrac{EPS}{bookequitypershare}$.

  ○ **Problems with this model.**

  ▪ Point estimations are always unspecific, better provide an interval with worst and best estimate.

  ▪ Estimations of r are always subject to errors, related to uncertainties in calculation of g.

  ▪ Analysts are subject to behavioral biases.

  ▪ RoE is subject to mean reversion.

- **RoE and mean-reversion.**

  ○ Mainly start-ups have high RoE at the beginning because there are lots of investment alternatives.

  ○ Calculating with an RoE of 20% will distort the future price and the related cost of equity.

  ○ Look at the data until the RoE "normalized" itself and then the real growth rate is revealed.

  → Look of sustainable growth.

  ○ To determine the present value of the stock, use the short cut formula for "t-period growing perpetuity".

  ○ Therefore the Present Value can be calculated by the following equation.

$$\overbrace{}^{\text{Specific growth}} \quad \overbrace{}^{\text{Constant growth}}$$

$$P_0 = \frac{DIV_1}{1+r} + \frac{DIV_2}{(1+r)^2} + \frac{DIV_3}{(1+r)^3} + \frac{1}{(1+r)^3} \times \frac{DIV_4}{r-.08}$$

=> Assumption of constant growth is often unrealistic.

- **Summary: How to calculate equity costs.**

  ○ (1) Estimate the future dividends.

  ○ (2) Calculate the firm's growth rate.

  ○ (3) Adjust the growth rate for the long-run.

  ○ (4) Determine the constant growth rate and cost of equity.

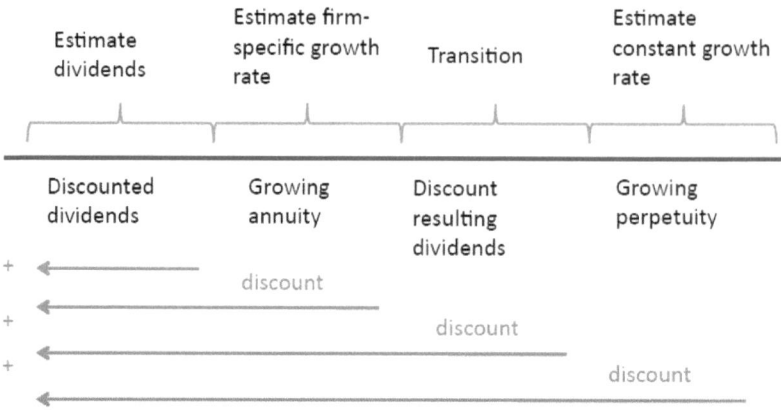

- **Growth Potential // PV of growth opportunities PVGO.**
  - ○ Comparison of one growing firm with itself in case of no growth.
  - ○ With growth, the fair price will be higher than in case of no growth.
  - ○ **PVGO = Growth value – Non-growth value.**
  - ○ Numerical Example.
    - ▪ Earnings of the firm are 8.33 € each period, expected return equals 15%, RoE is 25% and plowback ratio 40%.
    - ▪ Calculation of non-growth value: $\frac{Dividend}{r} = \frac{8.33}{0.15} = 55.56€$.
    - ▪ Calculation of growth value: $\frac{Dividend}{r-g} = \frac{Earnings*payoutratio}{r-(RoE*plowbackratio)} = \frac{8.33*0.6}{0.15-0.25-0.40}$.

$\frac{5}{0.15-0.1} = 100€$.

    - ▪ Calculation of PVGO $100 - 55.56 = 44.44$.

- **Conclusions.**
  - ○ If a firm has no growth, than it pays out all earnings as dividends.
  - ○ Investing in zero NPV projects, reinvesting will reduce dividends.
=> In both cases NPV is sum of discounted earnings.
  - ○ If firm is growing, dividends are decreasing now but then PV will increase.

- **Valuing Businesses.**
  - ○ **First approach: Free Cash Flow FCF**: Clean surplus, amount of capital can be paid out to investors.
→ Can be negative in case of start-ups.

- **General formula:** $P_0 = \sum_{t=1}^{\infty} \frac{FCF_t}{(1+r)^t}$.

- **Numerical Example:**

	1	2	3	4	5	6	7	8	9	10
Asset Value	10.00	12.00	14.40	17.28	20.74	23.43	26.47	28.05	29.73	31.51
Earnings	1.20	1.44	1.73	2.07	2.49	2.81	3.18	3.36	3.57	3.78
Investment	2.00	2.40	2.88	3.46	2.69	3.04	1.59	1.68	1.78	1.89
Free Cash Flow	-.80	-.96	-1.15	-1.39	-.20	-.23	1.59	1.68	1.79	1.89
EPS growth (%)	20	20	20	20	20	13	13	6	6	6

- After the 6th period, the growth rate is sustainable (simple pattern recognized).
- Calculate the PV of the first 6 periods, and then use the short-cut for the rest.

$\rightarrow$ 7th period is terminal year / horizon value.

- $PV(horizonvalue) = \frac{1}{(1.1)^6} * \left(\frac{1.59}{0.1-0.06}\right) = 22.4.$
- $PV(FCF) = -\frac{0.8}{1.1} - \frac{0.96}{(1.1)^2} - \frac{1.15}{(1.1)^3} - \frac{1.39}{(1.1)^4} - \frac{0.2}{(1.1)^5} - \frac{0.23}{(1.1)^6} = -3.6.$
- $PV(business) = PV(FCF) + PV(horizonvalue) = -3.6 + 22.4 = 18.8.$

- **Second approach: Based on P/E ratios.**
  - Take the same formula as before, but now use earnings instead of FCF.
  - $PV(horizonvalue) = \frac{1}{(1.1)^6} * (11 * 3.18) = 22.4$ If investor sells when P/E equals 11 (info is given)
  - $PV(business) = PV(FCF) + PV(horizonvalue) = -3.6 + 18.5 = 14.9.$

- **Third approach: Based on Market-Book ratios.**
  - Take the asset value of the 6th year, the year before the terminal year, and multiply it with the concatenator business market-book ratio (given; in this case: 1.4).
  - $PV(horizonvalue) = \frac{1}{(1.1)^6} * (1.4 * 23.43) = 18.5.$
  - $PV(business) = PV(FCF) + PV(horizonvalue) = -3.6 + 18.5 = 14.9.$

- **Fourth approach: Based on PVGO.**
  - Due to competition, the PVGO is mean-revert and the point in time at which it become zero, this reveals the company value.
  - **Given information:** The industry average for competition to catch up (here 9 periods).
  - $PV(horizonvalue) = \frac{1}{(1+r)^8} * \frac{earningsin.period9}{r} = \frac{1}{1.1^8} * \frac{3.57}{0.1} = 16.7.$
  - $PV(business) = PV(FCF) + PV(horizonvalue) = -2 + 16.7 = 14.7$

- **Which approach to use?**
  - Use them all to give a confidence interval because all are sensitive to single numbers.
  - Valuation bases on forecasts and heuristics / observations; haven't to be correct.

- **Source and Use of Funds.**
  - **Cash Cycle.**
    - Private households deposit their cash in banks, which will invest in companies.
    - Companies issue equity or debt to financial markets and private households can invest in this.
$\rightarrow$ Investments in firms can lead to real investments or financial assets.
  - Internal fund raising (Retained Earnings) is most common.
  - **Pecking Order Theory**: Companies prefer to finance new projects internally over issuing debt. Issuance of equity is the least-preferred method because this would raise bad signals about the firm.
  - **Different Debt Ratios.**
    - $bookdebtratio: \frac{LT.debt}{LT.debt+equity}$.
    - $bookdebtratio' = \frac{LT.liabilities}{LT.liabilities+equity}$.
    - $bookdebtratio'' = \frac{LT.liabilities}{TotalAssets}$.
    - $marketdebtratio = \frac{LT.liabilities}{marketequity}$ market equity = FV of outstanding shares.
=> All will reveal different values, be aware of how this numbers are computed and maybe adjust them.
  - **Equity.**
    - $Equitybookvalue = \frac{totalequity}{sharesoutstanding}$.
    - Market value per shares is the share price, observable at stock exchanges.
    - $Marketvalueto.bookvalue = \frac{marketcapitalization}{totalequity}$.

- **Different Types of Shares.**
  - A-shares, common shares.
    - Have the four basic rights of stockholders.
  - B-shares, preference shares.
    - No controlling rights, but superior cash flow rights.
$\rightarrow$ Hybrid instrument of debt and equity.
  - Average differences in both share-type prices reveals the price for controlling rights.
$\rightarrow$ Voting premium.
  - National differences, height reveals how much the people are willing to pay to direct the company to their own benefit.
  - "*Tunnelling*" to get something in return.

- Normally common shareholders are very interested in maximizing shareholders value because they receive only the rest of the net income.

→ High voting premium reveals that preference stockholders don't trust common shareholders that much.

- **Different Types of Bonds.**
  - Asset-backed bonds are normally more secure than debentures and therefore have higher priority and cash flow rights.
  - Debentures are bonds only secured by creditworthiness and more risky for investors.
  - **Special kinds of company bonds.**
    - Senior vs subordinated bonds: pecking order in case of bankruptcy.
    - Convertible bonds: Bonds can be turned into shares.
    - Callable bonds: Company can call bonds back before maturity.
    - Putable bonds: Investor can sell to company before maturity.
    - Sinking funds: Company sets cash aside to repay bond before maturity.
  - **Rating agencies grades.**

Moody's	S&P	Quality of Issue
Aaa	AAA	Highest quality. Very small risk of default.
Aa	AA	High quality. Small risk of default.
A	A	High-Medium quality. Strong attributes, but potentially vulnerable.
Baa	BBB	Medium quality. Currently adequate, but potentially unreliable.
Ba	BB	Some speculative element. Long-run prospects questionable.
B	B	Able to pay currently, but at risk of default in the future.
Caa	CCC	Poor quality. Clear danger of default .
Ca	CC	High specullative quality. May be in default.
C	C	Lowest rated. Poor prospects of repayment.
D	-	In default.

- **Issuing Securities.**

- **Venture Capital.**
  - Counted as equity because the provider receives controlling rights to prevent moral hazard.
  - VC is provided in several steps to minimize risk.
    - Seed financing: Develop a prototype.
    - Start-up financing: Beginning sales.

- Expansion.
- Bridge financing: Preparation of IPO.
  - **Main differences of Private Equity and Venture Capital.**
    - National differences.
      - In Germany both terms are synonyms.
      - In the US private equity is the general term, venture capital is more precise for the seed phase, for firms with high growth potential and risk.
  - More than half of the European VC investments generate a negative return, but still the mean excess return is very high (66.5%).
→ Enough risk compensation to let VC companies take the risk.

- **Initial Public Offerings IPO.**
  - **IPO**: First time the company offers shares to the market.
  - **Underwriter**: Connection between issuer of the security and public.
  - **Lead Underwriter**: Investment bank acting as underwriting syndicate.
  - **Gross Spread**: Provision for the Underwriter.
  - **Prospectus**: Information provided in case of an IPO.
  - **Underpricing**: Issued assets are underpriced and increase by high demand.
  - **Motives to go public.**
    - Use shares in future acquisitions.
    - Establish the market price of a firm.
    - Enhance overall reputation.
    - Minimize the cost of capital.
  - **Three ways to sell shares in an IPO.**
    - (1) **Fixed price offerings** (Germany, UK): Offer a fixed price for the shares and let them be bought.
    - (2) **Bookbuilding method** (most common): Perform a market survey, offer a price variety and let potential investors state their willingness to pay to calculate optimal price.
    - (3) **Auctions**.
      - **Second Price Auctions**: Highest bidder can buy shares for the price of the second highest bidder.
      - **Discriminatory Auctions**: Every bidder pays his bidding price, only to the highest bids will be sold.
      - **Uniform Price Auctions**: Quantity and price is submitted, company calculates who gets something regarding the height of the bids, who not, and then every one has to pay the price

of the lowest bid.

- **The IPO Process.**
  - (1st phase) Planning & Preparation: Recruit advisers and banks.
  - (2nd phase) Structuring: Due Diligence and Preparation of Prospectus.
  - (3rd phase) Realization and Marketing: Analysts presentation, research, finish & distribute prospectus.
  - (4th phase) Price Determination: Do the IPO.

- **Underwriters as a Certification Device.**
  - Underwriter should solve the asymmetric information between issuer and investor.

→ Signal of credibility.

  - **Criteria to hire an Underwriter.**
    - High overall reputation.
    - Diverse investor client base.
    - Industry's experience and connections.

- **Cost of Going Public.**
  - **Gross Spread:** Fee for the underwriter (buys low, tries to sell high).
  - **Additional direct costs**: Fees for consultants, lawyers, etc.

→ Both decrease proportionally with increasing value of the underlying.

  - **Indirect Cost**: Can't be measured, e.g. time of top management.
  - **Underpricing**: Price below par, rational decision (see below).
  - **Greenshoe option**: Callback-feature, not working well, secures the underwriter, not the issuer.
  - **Abnormal announcement return**.

=> IPO is very costly (capital, time, effort).

- **IPO Underpricing (aspect of information asymmetry).**
  - Issuance of assets on the primary market for a fixed price, but the secondary market will increase this price by trading.
  - **How to calculate the effect of underpricing.**
    - $Underpricing = \frac{closing price - offering price}{offering price}$.
    - $Money left. on the table = amount of shares * underpricing$.

=> Lost profits due to underpricing.

    - Nearly all companies do underpricing, on average 20%, in the extreme case 166% in China.

- ◦ **Explanation for underpricing – Winner's curse.**
  - ▪ Rational explanation of underpricing, but also theories for irrational behavior are true.
  - ▪ Key assumption is that there is a information asymmetry and problem of averse selection arises; many investors don't have the time to do high-quality analysis.
  - ▪ **Two kinds of investors**: uninformed (don't know future cash flows) and informed ones, last ones have more information than the underwriter (no uncertainty, know the future).
    - • Demand of uninformed investors is fixed, demand of informed ones depends on future development.
    - • Reasons to be more informed than the underwriter: (i) insider information, (ii) more experience, (iii) better intuition, (iv) better analysis tools.
  - ▪ Use the ration system (shares pro rata): If supply is lower than demand, set up the proportions of demand and distribute supply respectively.
    - • 100 shares available, one group wants to have 50, other 100, so group one becomes 1/3 of 100 and group 2 2/3 of 100.
  - ▪ (1) Estimate the possible future cash flows and weight them.
  - ▪ (2) Determine the demand of both kinds of investors.
  - ▪ (3) Set up a scenario analysis (pov of uninformed investor).
    - • Calculate expected return for each case.
  - ▪ (4) Sum up all scenarios and let them equal 0 to determine the optimal issuing price.
  - ▪ (5) Compare optimal issuing price with expected return and determine underpricing.
  - ▪ **Numerical example.**
    - • Equally likely possible outcomes are 120 or 80, so expected share price is 100.
    - • In case of 80, uninformed investors get 100 shares, in case of 120, they only get 66.66 ones.
    - • Case 1: $Return = \frac{2}{3} * (120 - P_0)$ Case 2: $Return = 1 * (80 - P_0)$.
    - • Optimal price: $\frac{0.5*2}{3} * (120 - P_0) + 0.5 * 1 * (80 - P_0) = 0 \rightarrow P_0 = 96$.
    - • Underpricing: $100 - 96 = 4$ in total 4 * 100 shares = 400 CU.
- => Only underpricing if case 1 (the most lucrative) has lower proportion than other cases.

- • **Rights Issues (aspect of fairness)**
  - ◦ In case of SEO there will be a dilution of voting rights because normally new shares are sold with a discount (DB sold for 35% less) → Old investors will lose money.
  - ◦ Right of preemption is mandatory in Germany (§ 186 AktG).
    - ▪ Related to the proportion of shares an old shareholder already holds, he has the right to buy the exactly proportion of new shares.

- This subscription rights should compensate old investors for the lower share price either by having new shares or by selling it and receive cash directly.
  - **Numerical Example – No rights issue.**
    - Current market capitalization: shares outstanding (20m) x FV (50) = 1,000.
    - SEO value: new shares (5m) * issuance price (40) = 200

→ Total market capitalization = 1,200.
    - Price per share after SEO $\frac{market\,capitalization}{amount\,of\,shares} = \frac{1,200m}{25m} = 48$.

→ Share price decrease of 2 CU, new share holders will benefit from this and face directly a gain of 8 CU per share.
  - **Numerical Example – Rights issue.**
    - Calculate the rights ratio RR $= \frac{old\,shares(20m)}{new\,shares(5m)} = 4:1$.
    - Value of one right $\frac{share\,price\,after\,SEO - issuance\,price}{RR} = \frac{48-40}{4} = 2$.

→ Rights valued at 2 CU each are distributed to old shareholders (get shares for free or can sell this rights to get the 2 CU directly).
    - New shareholders have to buy rights to be allowed to buy shares.

→ Total wealth distribution is 0, every investor is as well-off as before.

- **Payout Policy.**
  - Two kinds of wealth distribution to shareholders: Dividends and stock repurchases.
  - After the 1990s, the total amount and volume of repurchases of companies constantly increased.
  - **Dividend Payment Procedure.**
    - (1) Declaration Date: Company declares to pay out dividends at a specific day.
    - (2) Ex-dividend Date: Until now investors trade this share, price is rising.
    - (3) Record Date: All investors holding shares of this company are recorded to receive the dividend soon; after this share price drops by amount of dividend.
    - (4) Payment Date: Finally dividends are paid to investors.
  - **Reasons the amount of dividends is influenced by.**
    - Company tries to avoid reducing dividends and maintain a smooth stream of dividends.
    - Avoid a reduction because is gives negative signals to the financial markets.
    - Cost of external capital influences dividend amount.
  - Dividends and stock repurchases aren't substitutes.
    - Purchases: If company has large amount of cash collected and wants to change it's capital structure.

- Unlike dividends, repurchases aren't orientated at historic ones and haven't to be adjusted for the market.
  - ◦ For some time repurchases are permitted by the law.
    - Result was managers who tend to invest in very low return projects and shareholders didn't see any of the profit.

→ Therefore government regulation is about to change.

- **Correlation between Payout Policy and Company's Value.**
  - ◦ In case of (i) no taxes, (ii) no transaction costs, and (iii) fixed investments, financing and operating policies, the payout policy of a company doesn't influence its value.

=> Irrelevance Proposition of Miller & Modigliani (1961).

  - ◦ **Very easy numerical example.**
    - A fully-equity financed company will dissolve in t_1, but before that two cash flows of 100.000 each will occur with certainty (discount rate = 10%).
    - Company's value: $100,000 + \frac{100,000}{1.1} = 190,909.1$.
    - In case of 1,000 shares, fair share price: $\frac{100,000}{100} + \frac{\frac{100,000}{1.1}}{100} = 190.9$.

→ In case of 100% payout, the investors will get 190.9 CU per share hold.

    - **Scenario 1**: Suppose the company want to increase the amount of dividends for period 0 by 10%.
      - No debt can be borrowed, therefore raise other equity of 10,000.
    - New investors will only invest if they receive a dividend in period 1 amounted at 10%.
    - Hence, there is 100,000 in total and new investors claim for 11,000; the rest 89,000 can be distributed among old investors.

$110,000 + \frac{100,000-11,000}{1.1} = 190,909.1$ => Payout policy hasn't changed company's value.

    - **Scenario 2**: Suppose the company wants to perform a stock repurchase.
    - At a share price of 190.9 each, the company will buy 524 shares in period 1.
    - For the remaining shares, the dividend in period 1 is $\frac{\frac{100,000}{1.1}}{1,000-524} = 190.9$.

→ The investors subject to the stock repurchase get the same amount per share than the investors holding the shares until the end of the company.

=> In this simple setting, payout policy doesn't affect companies value.

  - ◦ **More intuitive approach to understand the Irrelevance Proposition.**
    - Investors can either have consumption needs or not (in case of investing all wealth into the company), and company could payout or not.

- If the company pays out dividends and the investor need this capital, her total value of shares will decline.
- If the company won't payout, investor who is in need of capital, will sell some stocks to satisfy her daily needs and total amount of shares will decline.
- If the investor has no consumption needs, we will either reinvest her dividends received to balance the loss in value related to the dividend or will do nothing if the company doesn't payout.

		Payout	
		Yes	No
Consumption	Yes	■ Shareholder (A) consumes dividend ■ Firm will finance investment through new shares ■ F sells shares with expected return r_E to new shareholders ■ Share of A declines	■ A sells shares to consume ■ F will finance investment through retention ■ A sells shares with expected return r_E to new shareholders ■ Share of A declines
	No	■ A reinvests dividend at rate r_E ■ Firm will finance investment through new shares ■ A will make use of his rights in the offering ■ Share of A remains unchanged	■ A does not do anything ■ Firm will finance investment through retention ■ Share of A remains unchanged

=> Payout policy doesn't matter, only the consumption needs of investor.

- **Other (more sophisticated) Theories on Payout Policy.**
  - **Rightists**: Prevent managers from overinvesting by paying out dividends.
    - If there is too much cash within the company and only bad investment alternatives (negative NPV) are available, managers tend to invest in such negative NPV projects.
    - By paying out the cash as dividend, the shareholders value would be increased by exactly the amount of loss the company would face if investing in the negative NPV project.
  - **Leftists**: If dividends are taxed higher than capital gains, paying out dividends would reduce shareholders value.
    - To reach the same after-tax rate of return, the companies initial share price must be lower.

	Firm A (No Dividend)	Firm B (High Dividend)
Next year's price	$112.50	$102.50
Dividend	$0	$10.00
Total pretax payoff	$112.50	$112.50
Today's stock price	$100	$97.78
Capital gain	$12.50	$4.72
Before-tax rate of return	$100 \times \left(\frac{12.5}{100}\right) = 12.5\%$	$100 \times \left(\frac{14.72}{97.78}\right) = 15.05\%$
Tax on dividend at 40%	$0	$.40 \times 10 = \$4.00$
Tax on capital gains at 20%	$.20 \times 12.50 = \$2.50$	$.20 \times 4.72 = \$.94$
Total after-tax income (dividends plus capital gains less taxes)	$(0 + 12.50) - 2.50 = \$10.00$	$(10.00 + 4.72) - (4.00 + .94) = \$9.78$
After-tax rate of return	$100 \times \left(\frac{10}{100}\right) = 10.0\%$	$100 \times \left(\frac{9.78}{97.78}\right) = 10.0\%$

- **Clientele Effects** arises: Even though dividends are higher taxed and investors will get lower returns, some investors prefer to invest in dividend paying companies.
  - Theorem states that low-income investors want to increase their yearly earnings by investing into companies and therefore need dividends.
    - High-income investors don't need additional income, therefore invest in growth companies to sell the shares and receive capital gains.

=> Firm can't benefit by increasing its dividends because investors have huge investment alternatives, an additional one won't increase the demand.

- **Dividend Signalling.**
  - Paying out dividends is mostly related to information asymmetry.
    - Dividends as signal of future prospect of the firm sent by investors who knows the firm best.
    - Increase in dividends send good news about increasing earnings to the market.
    - Dividend reduction is associated with trouble in the firm and declining earnings are supposed.

- **Transformation of the Balance Sheet.**
  - Accounting view of the balance sheet has to be transformed into the financial one.
  - Subtracting Payables from the current assets to receive the *Net Working Capital*.
    - NWC = Inventories + Receivables – Payables.
  - Subtracting Cash from the financial debt to receive the *Net Debt*.
→ Cash can be used to repay debt.
=> NWC + Net Debt = Operating Asset // Capital Employed.
=> Financial balance sheet only reveals market values, not book values (will balance because every asset generating no revenue is excluded).
  - **Enterprise Value** = Equity (FV) + Net Debt (FV) = FV of the capital employed.
→ Value of the whole firm.

- **Two Basic Principles for Company Valuation.**
  - ○ First: Firm needs to employ capital to generate a return and create value.
  - ○ Second: Each unit of capital invested has a certain cost.
    - ▪ Cost of Debt: Interest rate.
    - ▪ Cost of Equity: Requested risk compensation.
- => WACC as total capital cost has to be lower than the profit margins.

- **Weighted Average Cost of Capital (WACC).**
  - ○ After tax value (interest is tax deductible), but in a perfect capital market there is no tax.
  - ○ $WACC = \frac{E}{E+D} * r_E + \frac{D}{E+D} * r_D * (1 - taxrate)$.
  - ○ Cost of equity : Calculated by CAPM.
  - ○ $r_E = riskfreerate + equitybeta * marketriskpremium$.
    - ▪ Beta as quantity of risk, market risk premium as FV of risk.
  - ○ Cost of debt: $r_D = riskfreerate + defaultspread$(depending on company's PD).
  - ○ If capital structure is given $\left(\frac{D}{E} = k\right)$, than compute the portion of debt and equity by
    - ▪ $\frac{E}{D+E} = \frac{1}{1+k}and\frac{D}{D+E} = \frac{k}{1+k}$.

- **Numerical Example for Payout Policy.**
  - ○ Three firms with same operating asset to be liquidated at the end of this period.
  - ○ Generating profit by liquidation and by revenue of this period.
  - ○ All companies have a different capital structure and hence a different risk.
  - ○ Total Expected Cash Flows are {80, 120} (worst and best estimate).

	Equity	Debt		CF to E	CF to D
Firm A	100	0	Cash Flow of 80 occurs	80	0
Firm B	40	60		20	60
Firm C	10	90		0	80

  - ▪ Debt holders have the right for residual claim and are preferred over equity investors.
  - ▪ Because firm C can't provide the requested amount for debt holders, it will face bankruptcy problems.
- → Due to limited responsibility, there are no negative cash flows.
  - ○ Sum of this problem in two formulae.
    - ▪ $CashFlowto.equityinvestors = Max[0; EV - D]$.

- At least a CF of 0, maximum CF is enterprise value – net debt.
  - $CashFlow to. debtholders = Min[EV; D]$.
    - At maximum the net debt amount, at minimum the enterprise value.
=> Cost of equity is always higher than cost of debt (equity is riskier and has no upside limit).
  - **Does the capital structure matters?**
    - In a perfect capital market, replacing expensive equity by cheap debt will automatically increase the equity costs and in the end won't change the WACC (due to absence of taxes).
→ The higher the financial leverage, the higher the risk, the higher the equity costs.
  - **Company Valuation.**
    - Managers' overall goal is to maximize company's value (equal to minimize WACC).
    - $V = \sum_{t=1}^{\infty} \frac{EBIT_t}{(1+WACC)^t}$ => Maximization problem.

- **The Financial Leverage Effect.**
  - By borrowing cheaper capital instead of raising equity, there will be more capital remaining (after interest payments and repay of debt) to be spread among equity investors.
  - $RoE = \frac{CashFlow to. Equity Investors}{Equity}$ $RoE = RoA$(in case of no debt).
  - $RoE = RoA + \frac{D}{E} * (RoA - interest)$(in case of debt financed).
  - Return on equity can be calculated by $RoE = \frac{EBIT - interest * D}{Equity} = RoA + \frac{D}{E} * (RoA - interest) = r_A + I * (r_A - r_D)$.
→ The higher the leverage, the higher the return on equity (RoA will be amplified).
  - Equity risk is the sum of operational risk and financial risk and can be expressed by $\sigma_E^2 = (1 + I)^2 * \sigma_{ROA}^2$ <=> $\sigma_E = (1 + I) * \sigma_{ROA}$.
→ High leverage will amplify the operational risk (σ_{ROA}).

- **Example Leverage Effect.**
  - Two companies with same operational asset, but different capital structure.
  - In case of the fully-equity financed company, the RoE equals the RoA.
  - The partially debt financed company has a higher RoE as long as the RoA is greater than the debt interest rate (→ positive spread).
  - The "break-even" is either when RoA equals interest rate or when value of the levered and unlevered firm are equal (by given interest rates).

- **Modigliani & Miller Irrelevance Proposition.**

○ First: Some **assumptions** without the theory won't work.

- (1) Investors have the same expectations (model the future in the same way).

- (2) Operating asset is always given and the same, only focus on the capital structure.

- (3) We're acting in an perfect capital market.

  • Investors can't influence the market price, are price takers (= perfect competition).

  • Same interest rates.

  • Free access to all relevant information.

  • No transaction costs (can enter or leave the market without costs).

  • No individual or corporate taxes.

○ **The first MM Proposition.**

- Firm value is not affected by the capital structure, i.e. firm's WACC is not depend on it.

- Value of the firm is simply the value of debt and equity.

- Three assets in our market: Government bonds (risk-free), shares of unlevered firm and shares of the levered firm.

- Investors can set up portfolios with this assets.

- Identical portfolios have the same beta and have the same market price.

→ Law of one price, no arbitrage here.

  • In case of arbitrage: Buy low and sell high (no equity investment and risk-free profit).

- **First scenario.**

  • Buying 1% shares of unlevered firm → Claim for 1% of total profits.

  • Buying 1% of equity and 1% of debt of the levered firm → Claim for 1% of debt and equity profits = claim for 1% of total profits.

=> Because same return reveals that both companies are valued the same.

Investor buys a fraction of 1% of firm U's shares

Investment	Return
$0.01 \times V_U$	$0.01 \times$ Profits ←

Investor buys the same fraction of both debt and equity of firm L

	Investment	Return
Debt	$0.01 \times D_L$	$0.01 \times$ Interest
Equity	$0.01 \times E_L$	$0.01 \times$ (Profits - Interest)
Total	$0.01 \times (D_L + E_L)$	$0.01 \times$ Profits ←
	$= 0.01 \times V_L$	

Both strategies offer the same payoff!

Law of one price tells us that:
$$V_U = V_L$$

- **Second scenario.**

  • Buying 1% of levered firm's shares, claim for 1% of (profits – interest).

- Buying 1% of unlevered firm's shares with borrowed capital, claim for 1% of profits, but have to pay interest to the bank.

=> Same return reveals that both companies must have the same value due to the law of one price.

Investor buys a fraction of 1% of firm L's shares

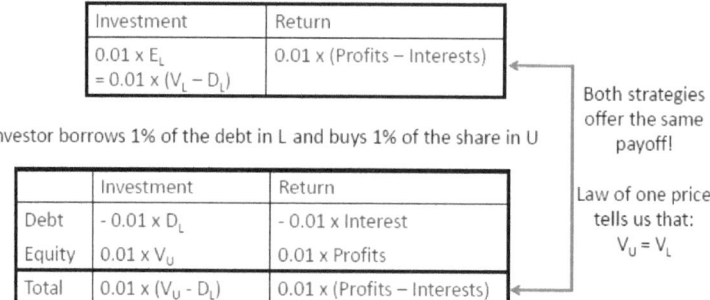

Investment	Return
0.01 x E_L = 0.01 x (V_L − D_L)	0.01 x (Profits − Interests)

Investor borrows 1% of the debt in L and buys 1% of the share in U

	Investment	Return
Debt	- 0.01 x D_L	- 0.01 x Interest
Equity	0.01 x V_U	0.01 x Profits
Total	0.01 x (V_U - D_L)	0.01 x (Profits − Interests)

Both strategies offer the same payoff!

Law of one price tells us that:
$V_U = V_L$

- **The second MM Proportion.**
  - **Homemade leverage.**
    - Leverage of the company has no effect on its overall valuation because investors can create their own "leverage" on their portfolio by finance it with debt.
    - When buying the shares of an unlevered firm with the same D/E ratio as the levered firm, investors return is equal to the one of the levered firm (in case of equity financed portfolio).
  - **Homemade deleverage.**
    - If investor sets up an fully-equity financed portfolio with the levered firm, he has the same financial and operational risk than the shareholders of the unlevered firm.

=> Investor can decide if he prefers leverage or not; or has access to an unlevered portfolio even though only levered firms existing.

  - **Mathematical formalization of MM1.**
    - When companies' value is not affected by leverage, cost of capital also won't be.
      - $WACC = \frac{E}{D+E} * r_E + \frac{D}{E+D} * r_D = r_{unlevered} = RoA$.
    - Direct relation between leverage and cost of equity can be found when solving this formula for $r_E = r_{RoA} + \frac{D}{E} * (r_{RoA} - r_{Debt})$.
      - Left term: risk without leverage, right term: additional risk due to leverage.
  - **Mathematical formalization of MM2.**
    - Cost of equity of a levered firm is equal to cost of equity of the unlevered firm plus an additional risk premium.
      - By increasing leverage, equity investors need / claim for further compensation for operational risk (r_{RoA}) and financial risk ($r_{RoA} - r_{Debt}$).

- **Beta and the leverage.**
  - Same formula for WACC only with related betas.
  - $\beta_{unlevered} = \frac{E}{D+E} * \beta_{Equity} + \frac{D}{E+D} * \beta_{Debt}$ Solving for β_{Equity} reveals
  - $\beta_{Equity} = \beta_{unlevered} + \frac{D}{E} * (\beta_{unlevered} - \beta_{Debt})$.
→ Leverage amplifies the market risk of a firm.
  - **Importance of the unlevered Beta.**
    - When comparing the individual risk of a project (equity beta), you need to have a starting point (unlevered beta) which you can adjust and align to this individual project.
    - Suppose there is one company from the telecommunication industry planing a new project.
      - First determine all similar firms in this industry, calculate their unlevered Beta with the formula above and take the average of it.
      - Start with the unlevered Beta and multiply it with 1+Capital structure to reveal the individual equity Beta for this project.
      - $\beta_{Equity} = \left(1 + \frac{D}{E}\right) * \beta_{unlevered}$.

- **Conclusions of MM Propositions.**
  - MM1: Companies' valuation is not affected by capital structure.
  - MM2: Cost of equity increases with the leverage, but lower debt cost will balance this effect.
→ Companies' value is primary driven by the enterprise value.
  - MM model represent the benchmark situation.
  - Most common violation of MM assumptions is corporate tax.

- **Numerical Examples regarding MM.**
  - (1) A company has a D/E-ratio of 2, current cost of debt 6% and cost of equity 12%; Company issues additional equity to repay part of its debt so new D/E ratio is 1 and cost of debt are reduced to 5.5%.
    - In case of perfect capital market, was is WACC and cost of equity after this transaction?
    - (a) Calculate WACC by $WACC = \frac{E}{E+D} * r_E + \frac{D}{E+D} * r_D$.
    - Remember that $\frac{E}{D+E} = \frac{1}{1+k}$ and $\frac{D}{D+E} = \frac{k}{1+k}$,
    - so $\frac{E}{D+E} = \frac{1}{3}, \frac{D}{D+E} = \frac{2}{3}$ and $WACC_{Before} = \frac{1}{3} * 0.12 + \frac{2}{3} * 0.06 = 0.08$.
    - (b) Due to MM1 we know that such transactions won't have an impact on companies' valuation and also on companies' WACC, therefore $WACC_{Before} = WACC_{After} = 8\%$.

- (c) Calculate the new cost of equity by $r_E = r_{RoA} + \frac{D}{E} * (r_{RoA} - r_{Debt})$.
  - $r_E = 0.08 + 1 * (0.08 - 0.055) = 0.105$.
- (2) Given the following data of telecommunication firms, how to explain the large differences in the equity betas? What beta to use for a valuation of a new project?

Name	Equity Beta	D/E ratio	Debt Beta
1	1.13	0.15	0.00
2	1.80	1.06	0.15
3	1.69	1.05	0.15
4	3.27	3.52	0.30
5	3.76	5.59	0.40

- Large difference in Equity Betas is related to financial risk rather than on market risk.
  - All companies are in the same industry, hence have a similar market risk.
  - Different financial leverages lead to a different equity beta due to $\beta_{Equity} = \beta_{unlevered} + \frac{D}{E} * (\beta_{unlevered} - \beta_{Debt})$.
- Best Beta for evaluation of new project? Unlevered beta, to be calculated by $\beta_{unlevered} = \frac{E}{D+E} * \beta_{Equity} + \frac{D}{E+D} * \beta_{Debt}$.
  - Results are within the range of 0.9 and 0.98, average is 0.938.
→ Use this as a starting point for project evaluation and do the adjustments as on $\beta_{Equity} = \left(1 + \frac{D}{E}\right) * \beta_{unlevered}$.

- **Consideration of Corporate Taxes.**
  - Corporate taxes will distribute the total cash flow to debt holders, the tax authority and the equity investors in that sequence.
  - FCF = CF (debt holders) + CF (equity investors) = EBIT – taxes.
  - Due to tax deduction, leverage will increase companies' value by PV of tax shield.
    - Tax shield: tax rate x interest payments.
    - CF (leverage) = CF (no leverage) + tax shield.
  - Comparison of tax deduction and no tax deduction.

	tax dedution	no tax deduction
EBIT	1250	1250
Interest	400	400
Tax (35%)	438 $\xrightarrow{-140}$	298
CF (equity investors)	412 $\xrightarrow{+140}$	562

- Additional increase in companies' value will go to equity investors.

$\rightarrow$ Preferential treatment makes debt even cheaper.

$\Rightarrow$ Break-down of MM 1.

- ○ **Detailed Example.**

  - Suppose the company has a constant EBIT and Debt over time, what will be the CF to equity investors?

  - CF (equity) = $(1 - tax) * (EBIT - interest * Debt)$ <=> $(1 - tax) * EBIT - interest * Debt + tax * interest * Debt$.

  - Equity value = $V_U - D + T * D = Value of unlevered firm - Debt + taxshield$.

  - PV of constant cash flows: $\frac{EBIT}{WACC}$ (in case of growth: $\frac{EBIT_1}{WACC-g}$ not EBIT$_0$).

  - Equity value first period: $\frac{(1-tax)*(EBIT-interest*Debt)}{cost of equity}$.

  - Equity value in case of no leverage: $\frac{(1-tax)*EBIT}{WACC}$.

  - PV of the tax shield in this case: $\frac{tax*interest*Debt}{interest} = Debt * Tax$.

$\Rightarrow$ Therefore value of levered firm: $V_L = E_L + D = V_u + tax * debt$.

$\rightarrow$ Levered firm is valued higher than unlevered firm, difference is PV of tax shield.

- ○ **Distinguish WACC into pretax and after-tax.**

  - $WACC_{aftertax} = \frac{E}{TA} * r_E + \frac{D}{TA} * r_D - \frac{D}{TA} * r_d * tax$.

$\rightarrow$ After-tax WACC will be lower than pretax WACC due to the tax deduction.

- ○ **Calculate the Present Value of the tax shield.**

  - Very difficult to calculate, except of two special cases.

    - Perpetuity: $PV(taxshield) = Debt * Tax$.

    - Constant D/E ratio: $V_L - V_U = \sum_{t=1}^{\infty} \frac{FCF_t}{(1+WACC(aftertax))^t} - \sum_{t=1}^{\infty} \frac{FCF_t}{(1+WACC(pretax))^t}$.

- **Combining Corporate Tax and Personal one.**

  - ○ Bondholders only pay personal tax on their interest revenue because such an interest expense is tax-free for the company.

  - ○ Shareholders have to pay personal tax and indirectly corporate tax.

  - ○ $CashFlow to. bondholders = Cash - T_p$.

- $CashFlow\,to.\,shareholders = (Cash - T_p) * (Cash - T_c).$

$\rightarrow$ Combining both cash flows will reveal the **relative advantage of debt** RAD.

- $RAD = \dfrac{cashflow\,bondholders}{cashflow\,stockholders} = \dfrac{Cash - T_p}{(Cash - T_p)*(Cash - T_c)}.$

  - Due to MM 1, RAD must be 1.
  - Related to different tax rates of capital gains, dividends and corporate taxes, nearly ever country has a different RAD.
  - Example for Germany: Dividends and capital gains are taxed with 25% + 5.5 % SolZ; assuming a corporate tax of 30% we get the following
  - $RAD_{Germany} = \dfrac{1-0.264}{(1-0.264)*(1-0.3)} = 1.43.$

$\rightarrow$ Main reason why in Europe most common way to finance firms is borrowing money.

- **Cost of Financial Distress.**
  - In case of illiquidity, the company doesn't automatically has to declare bankruptcy.
  - In case of delays, debtholders may claim for higher returns or interest premiums.

$\rightarrow$ Related to debt covenants, there are many costs arising.
  - Expected cost of default = likelihood of default * time of delay.
  - Therefore companies value = value of unlevered firm + PV of tax shield – PV of financial distress $\rightarrow$ **Trade-off** between gain and disadvantage of debt.
    - Unlevered firms value will stay constant over the the amount of debt.
    - Cost of financial distress will increase with increasing amount of debt, but also the value of tax shield.

$\rightarrow$ Highest point in the "actual value of the firm" line reveals optimal capital structure.
  - Profitable firms will have a high leverage because naturally their likelihood of default is lower.
  - Highly volatile cash flows have very high likelihood of default.
  - Companies with many tangibles will have a lower likelihood of default due to high liquidation value.[1]

---

[1] Image Source: https://image.slidesharecdn.com/chapter12capitalstructureconcepts-150222043955-conversion-gate01/95/capital-structure-concepts-chapter12-contemperary-financial-management-33-638.jpg?cb=1455270330

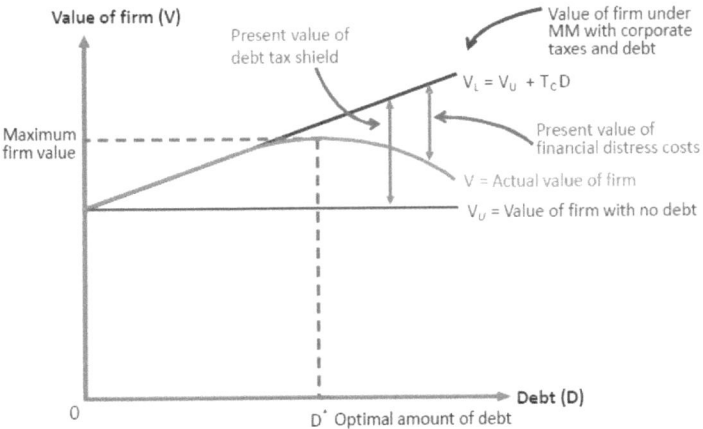

- **Bankruptcy Costs.**
  - Direct costs like administration or lawyer fees makes up to 5% of companies value.
  - Indirect costs are observed to make 20% of companies value and include fear of customers (claim for services), suppliers (won't deliver anymore) and **agency costs** (over- or underinvesting).
    - Either invest in negative NPV projects or invest not enough into profitable projects.
  - If the company is in the bankruptcy zone (value smaller than debt), market value will decline by bankruptcy costs.
  - **Deep Dive on agency costs.**
    - Having more debt and compensate managers with debt will reduce agency problems.
    - **(1) Asset Substitution Problem (result of overinvestment).**
      - Suppose a company is in financial distress, but has cash remaining to invest.
      - Equity investors have incentive to gamble and invest in negative NPV projects.
        - They won't face losses, worst case is getting nothing; therefore invest in such projects to increase expected value; they have nothing to lost.
        - High and unlikely cash flow is split between bondholders and shareholders respectively and expected value (cash flow x probability) higher than zero for equity investors.
  - → Debtholders will be harmed by this practice, but they are no managers, have no right to say.
    - **(2) Debt Overhang Problem (result of underinvestment).**
      - Suppose the same company found a lucrative investment opportunity, but don't have enough funds to do it.
      - Equity investors can invest more of their capital into the company to realize this project, but

this will only create value for bondholders; expected profit for shareholders is negative.

→ Equity investors won't invest even though this could prevent bankruptcy.

Asset Substitution Problem			Debt Overhang Problem		
	Bondholders	Shareholders		Bondholders	Shareholders
without gamble	200	0	without project	200	0
with gamble			with project		
win (10%)	300	700	initial outlay	0	-100
lose (90%)	0	0	payoff	300	50
expected value	30	70	total	300	-50

- **(3) Selfish Strategy of Milking the Company.**
  - Equity investors can also pay out the remaining cash as dividend to themselves, but debtholders will have secured themselves by the debt covenants.
- ○ **Conclusions.**
  - Equity investors don't care about the claims of debt holders.
  - The higher the leverage, the higher the temptation for equity investors to act for their own benefit.

- **Pecking Order Theory.**
  - ○ Based on asymmetric information, companies prefer internal financing over issuance of debt over issuance of equity.
  - ○ Suppose two companies with same market value, A is undervalued by the market, B overvalued.
    - If A wants to finance a new project externally, it won't issue shares because they are worth more, the don't want to give shares with such a high discount.
    - If B wants to finance a new project externally, they prefer equity for the same reason as above, but investors will wonder why B don't issue debt like A.

→ Investors assume that managers are hiding bad information and won't buy.

=> Result is that market value of B will align to intrinsic value in case of equity issuance.

- **Financial Slack.**
  - ○ Internal financing is the cheapest source of capital.
  - ○ Problems are: lower management effort and higher potential for private benefits.

- **Conclusion.**
  - ○ Both theories explain the debt- and equity decisions within a company.
  - ○ Four factors influencing this decision: size, tangibles, profitability and market-to-book ratio (higher MTB-ratio, lower debt).

- Pecking Order seems only to fit for large companies with access and experience to the bond markets.

- **Business Valuation – FCF Approach.**
  - $PV = \sum_{t=1}^{T} \frac{FCF_t}{(1+WACC)^t} + \frac{V_{terminal}}{(1+WACC)^t} NPV$ respectively.
  - Required is the FCF and an adequate discount rate (mostly the WACC).
    - FCF created by actual and future cash flow of operating asset, free from investment flow.
    - WACC has to be project-specific if the economic risk of the project deviates from the company's average.
  - **Two regime model**: one time span with very detailed forecasts, and terminal year.
    - Detailed forecast time span can be discounted the normal way, normally 3-8 periods.
    - Terminal year will be calculated by short-cut formulae.

$\rightarrow$ **Never forget to discount the terminal value again!**
  - FCF = EBIT – tax + depreciation & amortization – Δ Working Capital – CapEx.
    - Doesn't take tax deduction of interest into account because after-tax WACC is used to discount.
  - **Differences between FCF and Net Income.**
    - Net income is accounting based, after tax and interest, includes non-cash transactions.
    - FCF is cash flow for distribution among investors, captures the financial policy of the firm.
  - **WACC.**
    - Computed by risk free rate and risk premium (compensation for risk).
    - Captures economic risk (business activities) and financial risk (financial structure) of the firm.
    - Only use the WACC to evaluate company's new projects if the economic risk remains unchanged otherwise use a **project-specific WACC.**
      - Red flag is a NPV of 0, in such a case check the economic and financial risk of the project and compare it with those of the firm.

$\rightarrow$ Risk of this new project is only partially correlated to company's whole risk and in case of a big investment, will change the capital structure of the firm.
      - Calculate the WACC for this project by adjusting the equity beta, then the equity cost and then the company's WACC.
        - In a perfect capital market take the following formulae.
          - $\beta_{unlevered} = \frac{E}{D+E} * \beta_{Equity} + \frac{D}{E+D} * \beta_{Debt} \beta_{Equity} = \left(1 + \frac{D}{E}\right) * \beta_{unlevered}.$
        - In presence of taxes, use this one: $\beta_{Equity} = \left(1 + \frac{D}{E} * (1 - tax)\right) * \beta_{unlevered}.$

- **Conclusions from Valuing Cargo AG Example.**
  - Use the market values of operating assets and equity, but the book value of debt.
  - **Circularity Problem**: Firms market value is needed to compute the WACC, but market value of private firms can only be calculated by WACC.
    - Assuming a constant capital structure will solve this problem.
    - Not so unrealistic because companies have an optimal capital structure and CFOs will ensure this in the long-run, even if deviations occur in the short-term.
  - **How to compute the FCF.**
    - **Given information**: Sales; profit margin; depreciation, CapEx and working capital in relation to sales; terminal year; growth rate for both periods; tax rate.
      - Sales 4,000; short-term growth (till period 3) 4%; perpetual growth 3.5%; tax = 25%
      - Annual depreciation 5.3%; profit margin 10%; annual investment in PPE and working capital 10% each.
    - **Calculate the FCF with this information**.
      - Start all calculations in year 1, not zero, sales = 4,000 * 1.035 = 4,160.
      - Calculate EBIT = profits – depreciation.
      - Subtract taxes to get the NOPAT.
      - Calculate CapEx by change in PPE + depreciation.
      - Calculate changes in working capital.

=> FCF = NOPAT + depreciation – CapEx – Δ Working Capital.

	Year	0	1	2	3	4	5
(1)	Sales	4,000	4,160	4,326	4,499	4,657	4,820
(2)	EBITDA = 10% x (1)		416	433	450	466	482
(3)	**Depreciation** = 5.3% x **(1)**		220	229	238	247	255
(4)	EBIT = (2) - (3)		196	203	212	219	227
(5)	Taxes = (4) x T_c		49	51	53	55	57
(6)	**NOPAT** = (4) - (5)		147	153	159	164	170
	Net PPE = 10% x (1)	400	416	433	450	466	482
(7)	**CAPEX**		236	246	256	263	272
	WC = 10% x (1)	400	416	433	450	466	482
(8)	Investment in WC		16	17	17	16	16
(9)	**Free cash flow** = (6)+(3)-(7)-(8)		115	119	124	133	137

  - Don't forget to discount the terminal value again when calculating the PV_0.
  - When knowing the FV of the operating asset and assuming the FV of debt to equal the book value, we can calculate the equity of the company and have the financial balance sheet.

- **(I) Valuation of Stocks.**
  - **Expected return** = cost of equity capital = market capitalization rate.

$$\text{Expected return} = r = \frac{Div_1 + P_1 - P_0}{P_0}$$

  - **Future price** of stocks is present value of future cash flows.
    - In case of stocks: future value of dividends and ultimate sale price.

$$\text{Price} = P_0 = \frac{Div_1 + P_1}{1 + r}$$

    - Future price over multiple periods can be calculated by dividend discount model.

$$P_0 = \sum_{t=1}^{H} \frac{Div_t}{(1+r)^t} + \frac{P_H}{(1+r)^H}$$

    - H stands for the time period, the stock is sold.

→ The larger H, the less important the future price becomes, therefore neglectable.

$$P_0 = \sum_{t=1}^{H} \frac{Div_t}{(1+r)^t} + \lim_{H \to \infty} \frac{P_H}{(1+r)^H} = \sum_{t=1}^{\infty} \frac{Div_t}{(1+r)^t}$$

  - Shortcut formulae for share valuation.
    - Perpetuity: $P_0 = \frac{1}{r}$ If the same dividend is paid until infinity.
    - Growing perpetuity: $P_0 = \frac{1}{r-g}$ If the dividend is increasing by a fixed percentage g and paid until infinity.
    - t-period annuity: $\frac{1}{r} - \frac{1}{r*(1+r)^t}$ If the dividend is increasing by a fixed percentage g and paid until infinity, but only starting in a later period, before this constant pattern, there is something else.

- **(I.I) Estimating Equity Costs.**
  - $EquityCosts = r = \frac{Div_{\cdot 1}}{P_0} + g$ Dividend yield + growth rate.
  - Two ways to estimate the growth rate.
    - (I) Ask experts like Value Line or IBES.
    - (II) Calculate g by RoE x plowback ratio.
      - $plowbackratio = 1 - payoutratio. RoE = \frac{EPS}{bookequitypershare}$.

→ Be careful with g because subject to mean-reversion and experts subject to behavioral biases.

  - **Multi-period Valuation.**

- Suppose that a constant pattern (8% growth) is estimated after period 3, then calculate periods 1-3 by normal discounting.

- $P_0 = \left(\frac{DIV_{\cdot 1}}{(1+r)^1} + \frac{DIV_{\cdot 2}}{(1+r)^2} + \frac{DIV_{\cdot 3}}{(1+r)^3}\right) + \left(\frac{1}{(1+r)^3} * \frac{DIV_{\cdot 4}}{r - 0.08}\right).$

$\rightarrow$ Discounting + short-cut formula.

- **(I.II) Present Value of Growth Opportunities PVGO.**
  - Compare the share price with expected growth rate with the share price neglecting the growth rate (benchmark case).
  - $P_0(nogrowth) = \frac{Div_{\cdot 1}}{r}(g = 0$, payout ratio = 1); $P_0(growth) = \frac{Div_{\cdot 1}*(payoutratio)}{g - r}.$
  - $PVGO = P_0(growth) - P_0(nogrowth).$
  - If firm doesn't invest, earnings are paid out as dividends.

- **(II) Business Valuation.**
  - *(1) Valuation by Free Cash Flow (FCF).*
    - FCF: Capital available for distribution to investors (debt or equity); in case of start-ups often negative amount.
    - $FCF = cashflowfrom.operatingactivites - capitalexpenditures = earnings - investments.$
    - $V_0 = \sum_{t=1}^{\infty}\frac{FCF_t}{(1+r)^t}$in practice it is split into $V_0 = \sum_{t=1}^{H}\frac{FCF_t}{(1+r)^t} + \frac{PV_H}{(1+r)^H}.$
    - Similar to the valuation of stocks, after the terminal year (forecasted numbers won't change in future), short-cut formulae can be used.
    - Growth rate is the EPS growth rate; Suppose the following situation.

	1	2	3	4	5	6	7	8	9	10
Asset Value	10.00	12.00	14.40	17.28	20.74	23.43	26.47	28.05	29.73	31.51
Earnings	1.20	1.44	1.73	2.07	2.49	2.81	3.18	3.36	3.57	3.78
Investment	2.00	2.40	2.88	3.46	2.69	3.04	1.59	1.68	1.78	1.89
Free Cash Flow	-.80	-.96	-1.15	-1.39	-.20	-.23	1.59	1.68	1.79	1.89
EPS growth (%)	20	20	20	20	20	13	13	6	6	6

  - After the 6th period the EPS growth remains constant at 6%.
  - Hence: $PV(horizonvalue) = \frac{1}{(1+r)^{terminal}} * \left(\frac{FCF_{terminal}}{r - g}\right) = \frac{1}{(1.1)^6} * \left(\frac{1.59}{0.1 - 0.06}\right) = 22.4.$
  - Until the terminal year is reached, calculate by simple discounting of FCF.
  - $PV(FCF) = -\frac{0.8}{1.1} - \frac{0.96}{(1.1)^2} - \frac{1.15}{(1.1)^3} - \frac{1.39}{(1.1)^4} - \frac{0.2}{(1.1)^5} - \frac{0.23}{(1.1)^6} = -3.6.$

=> PV (business) = PV (FCF) + PV (horizon value) = -3.6 + 22.4 = 18.8.

- ○ **(2) Valuation by price-earning ratio.**
  - ▪ PV of horizon is calculated by discounted multiple of earnings, added to PV (FCF).
  - ▪ Needed information:
    - • Period when the company's earnings align to the industry's average (here: 6)
    - • Earnings at this period (here: 3.18).
    - • Selling price of company (multiple of earnings) (here: 11).
    - • FCF values for the periods before the terminal year (PV (FCF) = -3.6).
  - ▪ $PV(horizon value) = \frac{1}{(1+r)^{year}} * (multiple * earnings) = \frac{1}{(1.1)^6} * (11 * 3.18) = 19.7.$
  - ▪ $PV(business) = PV(FCF) + PV(horizon) = -3.6 + 19.7 = 16.1.$
- ○ **(3) Valuation by market-book ratio.**
  - ▪ Calculate the company's value by PV (FCF) + PV (horizon), but now the horizon is aligned to market-book ratio.
  - ▪ Needed information:
    - • Concatenator business market-book ratio and the respective period (here: 1.4 in year 6).
    - • Book value of this period (here: 23.43).
    - • FCF values before this period (PV (FCF) = -3.6).

$PV(horizon value) = \frac{1}{(1+r)^{year}} * (market - book ratio * earnings) = \frac{1}{(1.1)^6} * (1.4 * 23.43) =$

18.5.

  - ▪ $PV(business) = PV(FCF) + PV(horizon) = -3.6 + 18.5 = 14.9$
- ○ **(4) Valuation by PVGO.**
  - ▪ Under perfect competition growth is only a temporary phenomenon and will disappear one day.
→ Calculate the PV until this day and then use shortcut formula for the rest.
  - ▪ Needed information:
    - • Period in which competition catches up (here: 7).
    - • Earnings in that period (here: 3.18).
  - ▪ $PV(horizon value) = \frac{1}{(1+r)^{year}} * \left(\frac{earnings}{r}\right) = \frac{1}{(1.1)^6} * \left(\frac{3.18}{0.1}\right) = 17.95.$
  - ▪ $PV(business) = PV(FCF) + PV(horizon) = -3.6 + 17.95 = 14.35.$

- • **(III) Bonds & Shares.**
  - ○ **(1) Equity.**
    - ▪ Market to book value shares $= \frac{market capitalization}{total shareholders value}.$
    - ▪ A-Shares: common shares, 4 basic shareholder rights (dividend, vote, preemption,

liquidation).

- B-Shares: preference shares, not the 4 basic rights, superior cash flow rights.
- **Voting Premium**: Difference in price between price of A- and B-shares of one company.

→ Reveals the true value of voting rights, very different between countries and nations.

- **(2) Debt.**
  - **5 different kinds of (corporate) bonds.**
    - Senior vs subordinated bonds: pecking order in case of bankruptcy.
    - Convertible bonds: Bonds can be turned into shares.
    - Callable bonds: Company can call bonds back before maturity.
    - Putable bonds: Investor can sell to company before maturity.
    - Sinking funds: Company sets cash aside to repay bond before maturity.
  - **Bond Rating Grades.**

Moody's	S&P	Quality of Issue
Aaa	AAA	Highest quality. Very small risk of default.
Aa	AA	High quality. Small risk of default.
A	A	High-Medium quality. Strong attributes, but potentially vulnerable.
Baa	BBB	Medium quality. Currently adequate, but potentially unreliable.
Ba	BB	Some speculative element. Long-run prospects questionable.
B	B	Able to pay currently, but at risk of default in the future.
Caa	CCC	Poor quality. Clear danger of default .
Ca	CC	High specullative quality. May be in default.
C	C	Lowest rated. Poor prospects of repayment.
D	-	In default.

- **(IV) Initial Public Offering.**
  - **Motives to go public.**
    - Use shares in future acquisitions.
    - Establish the market price of a firm.
    - Enhance overall reputation.
    - Minimize the cost of capital.
  - **Cost of Going Public.**
    - **Gross Spread:** Fee for the underwriter (buys low, tries to sell high).
    - **Additional direct costs**: Fees for consultants, lawyers, etc.

→ Both decrease proportionally with increasing value of the underlying.

- **Indirect Cost**: Can't be measured, e.g. time of top management.

- **Underpricing**: Price below par, rational decision (see below).
- **Greenshoe option**: Callback-feature, not working well, secures the underwriter, not the issuer.
- **Abnormal announcement return**.

=> IPO is very costly (capital, time, effort).

- **Three ways to sell shares in an IPO.**
  - (1) **Fixed price offerings** (Germany, UK): Offer a fixed price for the shares.
  - (2) **Bookbuilding method** (most common): Perform a market survey, offer a price variety and let potential investors state their willingness to pay to calculate optimal price.
  - (3) **Auctions**.
    - **Second Price Auctions**: Highest bidder can buy shares for price of the second highest bidder.
    - **Discriminatory Auctions**: Every bidder pays his bidding price, only to highest bids will be sold.
    - **Uniform Price Auctions**: Quantity and price is submitted, company calculates who gets something regarding the height of the bids, and who not, and then every one has to pay the price of the lowest bid.
- **The IPO Process.**
  - (1st phase) Planning & Preparation: Recruit advisers and banks.
  - (2nd phase) Structuring: Due Diligence and Preparation of Prospectus.
  - (3rd phase) Realization and Marketing: Analysts presentation, research, finish & distribute prospectus.
  - (4th phase) Price Determination: Do the IPO.

- **(IV. II) Underpricing.**
  - Underpricing = closing price – offering price.

→ Market will determine the fair price very quickly.

  - Money left on the table: Underpricing per share x amount of shares issued.
  - **Winner's curse.**
    - Explain why underpricing seems to be a rational decision.
    - Required (simplifying) assumptions: **Information asymmetry** between (some) investors and underwriter.
      - Informed investors exactly know the future and will only invest in case of expected profit.
    - Lets reduce the possible outcomes to "beating expectations" and "missing expectations".
      - Demand of uninformed investors is always the same, in case of "missing expectations" 100%

of offered shares, in case of "beating expectations" 100% - % of informed investors.

=> Expected share price is the weighted average from both alternatives.

- Calculate the optimal price from the "uninformed investors" pov because they buy anyway.
  - Set up the equations for each of the both scenarios.
  - "Missing expectations": Return = 100% * (return for this case * price P)
  - "Beating expectations": Return = (100% - % of informed investors) * (return for this case * P).

→ Set up the weighted average and let it equal 0 to determine the optimal price.

=> Optimal price will be lower than expected price.

- **(IV. III) Rights Issue.**
  - Issuance of new shares (SEO) will normally happen for a lower price than actual shares' market price to encourage everyone to buy.
  - "Cheap" new shares will instantly decrease the old share price, but new market price will still be higher than issuance price → New investors will make high profits and old ones will be harmed.

=> To prevent this situation, rights issue is mandatory in many countries.

  - Situation without rights issue as benchmark.
    - $P_{new} = \frac{marketcapafterSEO}{totalsharesafterSEO} = \frac{oldamount*oldprice+newamount*issuanceprice}{oldamount+newamount}$.
    - $ValueperRight. = oldshareprice - newshareprice = P_{old} - P_{new}$.
    - Other possibility of calculation.
      - $Rightsratio = \frac{amountoldshares}{amountnewshares}$.
      - $ValueperRight. = \frac{newprice-issuanceprice}{RR}$.
  - Each "old shareholder" receives rights amounted at their shares held.
  - Either sell the rights or buy new shares to be compensated for the decreasing share price.

=> Rights are needed to buy the new shares.

- **(V) Payout Policy.**
  - **Miller and Modigliani's Irrelevance Proposition.**
    - Payout policy doesn't affect company value (later in more detail).
    - Required assumptions: (i) no taxes, (ii) no transaction costs, (iii) investment, financing and operating policies of the firm are constant.
    - If firm consists of two cash flows, its value is the discounted sum of both.
    - **Scenario 1: Distribute profits as dividends.**

- Due to the third assumption, the company will raise new equity if it wants to increase the dividends for their "old shareholders".
  - "New shareholders" claim for the same dividend rate than old shareholders, so increase in dividend this period and decrease in dividend next period will balance each other.

$\rightarrow$ Company's value is not affected by payout policy.

  - **Scenario 2: Distribute profits by repurchases.**
    - Suppose the cash flow of period 1 is used to repurchase some shares.
    - This reduces the amount of remaining equity investors, which claim for cash flow of period 2.

=> Company's value is not affected by this transaction.

  - **Intuition: Investors' consumption needs.**
    - Suppose the investor invested his initial wealth into the shares of one company.
      - If the company pays dividends, the investor uses them to finance his lifestyle.

$\rightarrow$ Value of the shares is reduced due to the dividend.

      - If the company pays no dividends, investor must sell some shares to finance his lifestyle.

$\rightarrow$ Value of the remaining shares stays the same, but portfolio of investor is worth less.

    - Suppose the investor only invested a part of his wealth.
      - If the company pays dividends, he buys more shares and the value of his portfolio stays constant.
      - If the company doesn't pay dividends, the value of his portfolio remains constant.

=> Portfolio value only depends on the circumstances of the investor, not on the payout policy.

  - **The Rightists.**
    - Dividends should be paid out to prevent managers from overinvesting.
    - Increase in companies value is the prevented loss.
  - **The Leftists.**
    - Don't pay dividends if they are taxed higher than capital gains; better repurchase them.
    - **Clientele Effect**: Low income investors nevertheless claim for dividends because they need to finance their lifestyle.

- **(VI) Transformation of the balance sheet.**
  - Left side: Fixed assets + Net Working Capital = Operating asset // capital employed.
    - NWC = Inventories + Receivables – Payables.
  - Right side: Equity + Net Debt = Enterprise Value.
    - D = Financial debt – cash.

=> All listed at market value, not book value anymore.

- ◦ Why turn accounting balance sheet into a financial one?
  - ▪ Valuation of firm only depends on their operating asset // enterprise value.
  - ▪ Reduce the business to their core activities (operations and capital structure).

- **(VII) The Financial Leverage Effect.**
- ◦ Equity is riskier than debt because in case of insolvency debt holders are preferred.
- ◦ Substitution of "expensive equity" with "cheap debt" won't decrease the WACC because the higher the debt, the lower the remaining equity, the higher the equity risk, the higher the equity cost → Due to MM 1 both effects will cancel out and WACC remains the same.
- ◦ $RoE = \frac{EBIT - interest * D}{Equity} = RoA + \frac{D}{E} * (RoA - interest) = r_A + I * (r_A - r_D)$
- ◦ Return on equity is subject to leverage effect: $RoE = RoA + \frac{D}{E} * (RoA - interest)$.
- ◦ Equity risk is also subject to leverage effect: $\sigma_E^2 = \left(1 + \frac{D}{E}\right)^2 * \sigma_{RoA}^2$.
- ◦ Leverage effect will boost good times, but also worsen bad times.
  - ▪ Debt is only advantageous if the interest rate is (way) lower the RoA.
- → Take (seasonal or unexpected) fluctuations into account.

- **(VIII) Miller & Modigliani's Irrelevance Proposition.**
  - ▪ Required assumptions:
    - • All investors have the same expectations.
    - • Operating asset of examined firms is the same, only capital structure differs.
    - • Perfect capital market.
      - ◦ Investors are price takers, can't influence the market, perfect competition.
      - ◦ Same interest rates for equity and debt, won't increase or decrease by quantity borrowed.
      - ◦ Access to all relevant information.
      - ◦ No transaction costs and taxes (neither personal nor corporate ones).

- **(VIII. I) Miller and Modigliani's Proposition 1 (MM 1).**
- ◦ Capital structure does not affect companies' value.
- ◦ **First situation.**
  - ▪ Buy 1% of shares of an unlevered firm (all-equity financed), allows to claim for 1% of profits.
  - ▪ Buy 1% of equity and 1% of debt of a levered firm, allows to claim for 1% of profits.
- => Due to the law of one price, both companies should have the same value.
  - ◦ **Second situation.**
    - ▪ Buy 1% of shares of levered firm, allows to claim for 1% of (profits – interest).

- Set up a portfolio of 1% of shares of an unlevered firm, financed by debt capital; portfolio return is 1% of company's profits – interest for capital borrowed.

=> Same result, due to law of one price, both companies should have the same value.

  ○ **Homemade (de-)leverage.**
  - Investors can arrange their own leverage level within their portfolio and fully control it.
  - Capital structure of a firm doesn't matter since the investor can realize his own preferences by borrowing capital or use own funds.

→ Since investors have the full control, companies' valuation can't be affected by capital structure.

  ○ **Mathematical formalization.**
  - Since companies valuation is not affected by capital structure and overall goal is maximization of shareholders value (either maximize profits or reduce (capital) costs), we can state:
  - $WACC = \frac{E}{TA} * r_E + \frac{E}{TA} * r_D = r_{unlevered} = RoA.$

- **(VIII. II) Miller and Modigliani's Proposition 2 (MM 2).**
  ○ Linear negative correlation between equity costs and financial leverage.
  ○ Solve the WACC formula for the equity costs (= RoE) and receive the following:
  ○ $RoE = RoA + \frac{D}{E} * (RoA - interest).$
  - Expected return to equity investors of a levered firm equals expected return of an unlevered firm plus an additional risk compensation.

→ Leverage increases the risk of equity investors.

=> Additional equity risk and reduced debt risk will balance and ensure always the same WACC.

- **(VIII. III) Beta and the Leverage.**
  ○ Goal is overall risk estimation / evaluation of new (special) projects of a firm.
  - We need a company specific anchoring point and an adjustment term to align company's risk to the new project.

  Due to MM 1 we can express company's overall risk by $\beta_{unlevered} = \frac{E}{D+E} * \beta_{Equity} + \frac{D}{E+D} * \beta_{Debt}.$

→ Use this unlevered beta as a anchoring point and adjust for the leverage effect.

  ○ With MM 2 we can make the following adjustment: $\beta_{Equity} = \beta_{unlevered} + \frac{D}{E} * (\beta_{unlevered} - \beta_{Debt}).$

=> When ever the company sets up a new project, the equity beta will change; by knowing the unlevered beta, adjustments can be made with observable information to quickly identify the new equity beta and calculate the optimal price.